AFFIRMATIVE
ACTION

Essential Viewpoints

AFFIRMATIVE ACTION

BY M.J. COSSON

Content Consultant
Teresa Nelson
Legal Counsel
ACLU of Minnesota

ABDO
Publishing Company

CREDITS

Published by ABDO Publishing Company, 4940 Viking Drive, Edina, Minnesota
55435. Copyright © 2008 by Abdo Consulting Group, Inc. Intenational copyrights
reserved in all countries. No part of this book may be reproduced in any form without
written permission from the publisher. The Essential Library™ is a trademark and
logo of ABDO Publishing Company.

Printed in the United States.

Editors: Paula Lewis, Patricia Stockland
Cover Design: Becky Daum
Interior Design: Lindaanne Donahoe

Library of Congress Cataloging-in-Publication Data

Cosson, M. J.
  Affirmative action / M. J. Cosson.
      p. cm. — (Essential viewpoints)
  Includes bibliographical references and index.
  ISBN 978-1-59928-857-4
  1. Affirmative action programs—Juvenile literature. 2. Minorities—
        Employment—Juvenile literature. I. Title.

  HF5549.5.A34C67 2007
  331.13'3—dc22

                                        2007013877

TABLE OF CONTENTS

Affirmative action is intended to provide equal opportunities to everyone.

LEVELING THE
PLAYING FIELD

Affirmative action means taking positive steps to increase the representation of minorities and women in jobs, education, and contracting. This pertains especially to areas in which minorities and women have been excluded in the past.

The intention of affirmative action is to provide equal opportunities for all and to right past wrongs. The phrase "leveling the playing field" is often used to describe the process.

Reverse Discrimination

Reverse discrimination is against whites or males, usually in employment or education.

However, leveling the playing field is not easy. Each situation is unique. As a consequence, over the course of many years, laws have been written and rewritten. Court cases have been argued, won, and then overturned. Quotas have been established that set a number or percentage of minorities that must be met in hiring practices and college admissions. These same quotas may later be overturned or changed by court order. In trying to follow guidelines, employers have misinterpreted and misrepresented affirmative action. Affirmative action has often been misunderstood.

Heart of the Controversy

For many people, affirmative action has been positive. However, others have felt that affirmative action has caused harm. The goal of affirmative action is to make sure that all people, regardless of race, gender, disability, or ethnicity, have the same opportunities.

In order to level something, it needs to be tipped slightly in one direction and then slightly in another direction until it is perfectly balanced. The scales of justice might seem to tip off-balance during the attempt to create a nation in which all people have a fair chance at realizing their potential. That is not the intention, but that is how laws regarding affirmative action have been viewed and interpreted.

Not only do affirmative action programs differ, but employers' interpretations of laws can differ also. Some programs might only review hiring processes for women and minorities. Other programs may be directed at hiring members of a specific minority group. Affirmative action represents the most recent in a long line of attempts to provide equality for every person.

ESTABLISHING FREEDOM FOR ALL

Not so very long ago, the scales of justice were tipped way off balance. The United States of America was built on the idea of freedom for all. In 1776, the new country prided itself in the freedoms that its citizens enjoyed. However, only in the past 150 years has the country focused on passing laws in an effort to treat all people fairly and equally.

The U.S. Constitution was ratified in 1788. The Bill of Rights was added to the U.S. Constitution in 1791. Those who shaped the government and these documents were intent on freeing the colonies from the King of England. Freedom to worship had brought the pilgrims to new shores, and those who followed fought for this and other freedoms. The words in the U.S. Constitution and Bill of Rights were carefully chosen to ensure the common man was represented. Women and those enslaved, however, were not considered. Slavery continued in the United States for nearly another 100 years. It was legal until 1865, when the Thirteenth Amendment to the U.S. Constitution officially abolished slavery. Women's rights took even longer to establish. In August 1920, the Nineteenth Amendment was signed into law, giving women the right to vote. Despite these amendments, African American men and all women still had to fight for equal treatment in society.

Jim Crow Laws

In southern states, Jim Crow laws were established as a reaction to the abolishment of slavery. Jim Crow laws kept a number of public areas and activities separated, based solely on race.

In Florida, separate schools were established for white children and black children. In Georgia, black barbers were not allowed to cut the hair of white women or girls. Also in Georgia, black deceased and white deceased people were not allowed to be buried in the same areas of graveyards.

Brown v. Board of Education: Separate but Equal

For decades, white children and African-American children attended separate public schools in America. The 1896 U.S. Supreme Court ruling in *Plessy v. Ferguson* established the separate but equal principle to segregate public schools. The black schools in Topeka had equal facilities and teacher salaries. There were 18 elementary schools for whites and only four for African Americans. The Topeka schools had provided its black students with facilities. It refused to upset its white residents by enrolling African-American children in neighborhood schools.

The Rights of Citizenship

The Civil Rights Act of 1866 gave the rights of citizenship to all men. In 1868, the Fourteenth Amendment granted citizenship to every man born in the United States. It also prohibited any state from denying "life, liberty, or property without due process of law."[1] And, it guaranteed equal protection under the laws. In 1870, the Fifteenth Amendment gave free men the right to vote. Women were not included in these acts.

The Civil Rights Act of 1875 guaranteed all men equal access to public accommodations, regardless of race or color. In 1896, Homer Plessy, an African-American man from Louisiana, challenged the constitutionality of segregated railroad coaches. In *Plessy v. Ferguson*, the U.S. Supreme Court legitimized segregation by stating that "separate but equal" accommodations were constitutional.

BROWN V. BOARD OF EDUCATION: SEPARATE IS NOT EQUAL

The separate but equal principle was often unfair and lacked equality. With the help of the National Association for the Advancement of Colored People (NAACP), many African-American parents filed lawsuits.

In 1951, *Brown v. Board of Education* was filed by the NAACP in Topeka, Kansas, on behalf of 13 parents. These parents wanted equal opportunities for their children. The schools and academic opportunities for African-American children were often inferior to those for white children. In some instances, African-American children were not provided buses, while white children were bussed to school. Programs and textbooks were not equally available to black schools.

The Abolition of Slavery

The Thirteenth Amendment was ratified on December 6, 1865, and includes, "Neither slavery nor involuntary servitude, except as a punishment for crime whereof the party shall have been duly convicted, shall exist within the United States, or any place subject to their jurisdiction."[2]

THE *BROWN* DECISION

The U.S. District Court ruled in favor of the school board. The NAACP appealed to the U.S. Supreme

Thurgood Marshall

Court. The case was initially argued by Thurgood
Marshall and other NAACP lawyers in December 1952.
The case was not argued on its own. *Brown v. Board of
Education* was combined with four similar NAACP cases.
Marshall and his team reargued these five cases one year
later. After much deliberation, the U.S. Supreme

Court delivered its landmark
decision on May 17, 1954:

> *We come then to the question presented:*
> *Does segregation of children in public*
> *schools solely on the basis of race, even*
> *though the physical facilities and other*
> *"tangible" factors may be equal, deprive*
> *the children of the minority group of equal*
> *educational opportunities? We believe*
> *that it does. … We conclude that in the*
> *field of public education the doctrine of*
> *"separate but equal" has no place.*
> *Separate educational facilities are*
> *inherently unequal. Therefore, we hold*
> *that the plaintiffs and others similarly*
> *situated for whom the actions have been*
> *brought are, by reason of the segregation*
> *complained of, deprived of the equal protection of the laws*
> *guaranteed by the Fourteenth Amendment.*[3]

NAACP

The National Association for the Advancement of Colored People was founded in 1909. Members include people of many races and nationalities. The NAACP believes that all men and women are created equal and work toward protecting that equality. Their goal is to work for educational, social, political, and economic rights regardless of race or gender.

The decision in *Brown v. Board of Education* overturned
Plessy v. Ferguson. However, it did not end the struggles
that many African-American children faced in public
school. Over the years, other legal cases and the civil
rights movement helped integrate schools and other

public places. The ruling in *Brown v.
Board of Education* was a step in the right
direction, but much work for equality
was left to be done.

Women's Right to Vote

The Nineteenth Amendment was ratified on August 18, 1920: "Section 1: The right of citizens of the United States to vote shall not be denied or abridged by the United States or by any State on account of sex. ... Section 2: Congress shall have power to enforce this article by appropriate legislation."[4]

Newly integrated classes at Springer, Oklahoma, on August 29, 1958

Mema Beye, right, hugs Zeba Khan, both from Tufts University Fletcher School of Law and Diplomacy, before Tufts University's commencements on May 20, 2007.

SHOULD AFFIRMATIVE ACTION CONTINUE?

*A*ffirmative action has made great strides in leveling the playing field. Since affirmative action began, people have been asking themselves the same questions: Is it necessary? Is it time to stop affirmative action? Is affirmative action fair to everyone? Does affirmative action work? Opinions differ and many questions remain.

OPPOSED: DECISIONS SHOULD BE BASED ON MERIT

Can we find a better way to accomplish the goal of equality? Can we just accept everyone as an individual? As our world continues to shrink, society has become more diverse.

Affirmative action is not perfect. Busing and integration were imperfect tools that promoted equality. They, too, caused racial strife. Opponents to affirmative action feel that decisions about hirings and college admissions should be based on merit alone. Race should not be a factor. Only after race is elimintated from the decision process can a truly unbiased decision be made.

OPPOSED: AFFIRMATIVE ACTION IS NO LONGER NECESSARY

The African-American middle class is growing. The mean annual income in 2001 of African-American families with two parents was close to that of all other middle-class families. About 40 percent of all African-

American families with two parents are middle-class or higher. The black poverty rate has been cut in half since the Civil Rights Movement.

Because of this success, many feel that affirmative action has done its job. After all, opponents point out, if as many minorities receive the same advantages as whites, it would be unfair for minorities to receive additional advantages through affirmative action.

In Favor: Minorities Are Underrepresented

How can affirmative action work when it does not include everyone? Private companies with fewer than 50 employees are exempt from affirmative action regulations. These smaller employers employ about one-third of all American workers. In 1994–1995, the Labor Department's Office of Federal Contract Compliance Programs found that 75 percent of the employers it checked were not in compliance with affirmative action. If only 25 percent of companies comply with affirmative action rules, affirmative action cannot be expected to make a significant difference.

Even with affirmative action programs in place, white males still hold approximately 95 percent of the high-level corporate jobs. Between 1990 and 1994, only 100 out of 3,000 federal court cases involving

Patricia Ireland, president of the National Organization for Women (NOW)

discrimination were about reverse discrimination. Of those cases, only six claims were found to be valid. According to the National Organization for Women (NOW), if half of the people of color who were admitted to colleges and universities under affirmative action were cut, only two percent more white males would be accepted to those schools.

In Favor: Testing Is Unfair

The National Center for Education Statistics conducted a survey on U.S. dropout rates. According to their 2004 national survey, the dropout rate is:

❖ 10.4 percent for students from low-income families.

❖ 8.9 percent for Hispanic students.

❖ 5.7 percent for African-American students.

❖ 4.9 percent for students of mixed race.

The dropout rate is highest for minority and poor students. Because

---

Have We Done Enough?

In 1967, when affirmative action was in its infancy, President Lyndon B. Johnson had to respond to racial strife in Detroit and Newark. He believed that the United States needed to do everything in its power to gain equality for all people.

However, times have changed—or have they? The question today is: Have we done enough, or are there more reasons than ever to continue affirmative action and other tools to achieve a nation of equality?

Comparing 2006 to 1967
The following figures are from
U.S. Census Bureau data.

World Population

2006: 6.5 billion	1967: 3.5 billion

Coming to America

2006: 34.3 million foreign-born people. They comprise 12 percent of the total population.	1967: 9.7 million foreign-born people. They comprised 5 percent of the total population.

Percentage of Women in the Labor Force
(age 16 and older)

2006: 59 percent	1967: 41 percent

Percentage of the Population with at Least a High School Diploma (age 25 and older)

2006: 85.2 percent	1967: 51.1 percent

minorities continue to receive less education than their white counterparts, they are at a disadvantage. When employers use tests to determine abilities, it is unfair to the less educated minorities. Although employers may feel they are eliminating bias, tests often favor whites.

Understanding Affirmative Action

Creating equality for all is a difficult task. It needs many tools. It might be time to create new tools. Education and awareness of the value of all people go hand in hand with affirmative action. While society educates itself on how to create and apply equality, the debate over affirmative action's usefulness continues.

The arguments for and against affirmative action have been addressed since the policy began. These arguments have played a large role in shaping today's

Revealing Subconscious Biases

Jerry Kang, a UCLA law professor, has introduced a new method of testing people's subconscious biases, called "behavioral realism." Based on his findings, Kang notes that current tests and testing practices are not, in fact, "color blind." He had proposed new testing models that are based neither on previous affirmative action methods nor future predictions. Instead, he uses the term "fair measures." These are updates to affirmative action that Kang suggests would offer more social equality. Kang believes that fair measures are no longer needed in society when society's subconscious bias tests at zero.

affirmative action laws. In order to understand affirmative action, it is important to understand how it has been used in the past. By looking at its effects on previous generations, one can better understand its role in the present. ⌐

University of Arkansas Clinton School of Public Service graduates listen to the commencement address by former president Bill Clinton on December 13, 2006.

Women advertise a free rally on women's right to vote in Washington, D.C., on October 3, 1915.

The Early Days of Affirmative Action

The concept of affirmative action began with the anti-slavery movement more than two centuries ago. It grew from the abolition of slavery to voting rights for all people to the integration of schools and public places. Twenty years of desegregation followed the *Brown v. Board of Education* decision. Desegregation, or integration, meant that school boundaries had to be changed. To achieve this, systems for busing students to schools to achieve integration were planned and implemented. Desegregation continues to be an ongoing process.

With systems of integration in place, the job of leveling the playing field had just begun. Now it was time to continue the work of equality for all people— regardless of race, gender, or other factors. It was time to take affirmative action.

Historically, white males had been the recipients of the best educations. They often received preferential admission as the children of alumni. White males also held the highest paying jobs. In many states, laws barred women from employment in physically tough jobs such as mining, bartending, or fire fighting. Some states even barred women from the areas of law or medicine. African Americans worked in menial jobs or as bellboys or porters. African Americans who were fortunate enough to go to college usually attended all-black colleges.

Armed Forces

In July 1948, President Harry S. Truman signed Executive Order 9981. This order called for the desegregation of the armed forces.

When they graduated, some of the best jobs they could get were teaching positions at those same colleges. Hispanics, Asians, and other minorities encountered similar difficulties.

WORKING FOR EQUALITY

Opportunities for minorities and women opened up during World War II. On June 25, 1941, President Franklin D. Roosevelt issued Executive Order 8802. This order barred defense contractors from discrimination based on race, color, or national origin. The executive order also established the first Committee on Fair Employment Practices.

The order did not have any enforcement authority. During the war, there was a shortage of workers. Women and minorities took over jobs that previously had been denied to them. However, the jobs went back to white males after the war. By 1960, almost all of the 10 million workers at the 100 largest defense contractors were white males.

No Discrimination

At the beginning of World War II, President Franklin D. Roosevelt issued Executive Order 8802, which states: "I do hereby reaffirm the policy of the United States that there shall be no discrimination in the employment of workers in defense industries or government because of race, creed, color, or national origin."[1]

President John F. Kennedy delivering his inaugural address

Legislating Equal Rights

President John F. Kennedy first used the term affirmative action in an Executive Order on March 6, 1961. He issued Executive Order 10925 in response to the Civil Rights Movement. The order prohibited discrimination in federal government hiring based on race, religion, color, or national origin. The order also established the President's Committee on Equal Employment Opportunity (EEO).

Affirmative Action

Executive Order 10925 states: "The contractor will take affirmative action to ensure that applicants are employed, and that employees are treated during employment, without regard to their race, creed, color, or national origin."[2]

In June 1963, Congress passed the Equal Pay Act of 1963. This act protected men and women who did the same type of job for the same employer from wage discrimination based on gender. This was the first national legislation based on employment discrimination.

In the midst of the civil rights campaign of 1963, President Kennedy appeared on national television and proposed a civil rights bill. The bill would make discrimination in all public facilities illegal. It would also expand the Equal Employment Opportunity Committee and cut off federal funds to any institution that discriminated.

On June 19, 1964, the longest debate in the history of the U. S. Senate ended with the passage of the Civil Rights Act of 1964. On July 2, 1964, the Civil Rights Act was passed by the U.S. House of Representatives. President Lyndon B. Johnson signed the bill into law that evening.

The Civil Rights Act of 1964 is made up of 14 Titles (or sections):

❖ Title I addresses voting rights.

❖ Title II addresses discrimination in public places.

❖ Title III addresses desegregation of public places.

❖ Title IV addresses desegregation related to public education.

❖ Title V sets the duties for the Commission on Civil Rights.

❖ Title VI addresses nondiscrimination in federally funded programs.

❖ Title VII pertains to equal opportunity in employment. It focuses on ending discrimination based on race, color, religion, sex, or national origin by employers of 15 or more employees. Title VII also establishes the Equal Employment Opportunity Commission (EEOC).

❖ Titles VIII through XI deal with other matters related to civil rights.

Section 703 Under Title VII of the Civil Rights Act of 1964:

(a) It shall be an unlawful employment practice for an employer—

(1) to fail or refuse to hire or to discharge any individual, or otherwise to discriminate against any individual with respect to his compensation, terms, conditions, or privileges of employment, because of such individual's race, color, religion, sex, or national origin; or (2) to limit, segregate, or classify his employees or applicants for employment in any way which would deprive or tend to deprive any individual of

To Fulfill These Rights

On June 4, 1965, President Lyndon B. Johnson spoke to the graduating class at Howard University. His speech made it clear that affirmative action was needed—civil rights alone would not end discrimination.

… it is not enough just to open the gates of opportunity. All our citizens must have the ability to walk through those gates.

…We seek not just freedom, but opportunity. We seek not just legal equity, but human ability; not just equality as a right and a theory, but equality as a fact and equality as a result. For the task is to give 20 million Negroes the same chance as every other American to learn and grow, to work and share in society, to develop their abilities. …

[E]qual opportunity is essential, but not enough. Men and women of all races are born with the same range of abilities. But ability is not just the product of birth. Ability is stretched or stunted by the family that you live with and the neighborhoods you live in, by the school you go to and the poverty or the richness of your surroundings. It is the product of a hundred unseen forces playing upon the little infant, the child, and finally the man.[3]

employment opportunities or otherwise adversely affect his status as an employee, because of such individual's race, color, religion, sex, or national origin. [4]

President Lyndon B. Johnson also used the term affirmative action in Executive Order 11246, which he signed on September 24, 1965. This order required federal contractors to take affirmative action and set timetables in order to do business with the federal government. In 1967, Executive Order 11246 was amended to include women.

In 1967, Congress passed the Age Discrimination in Employment Act. It protected people in the age bracket between 40 and 65 from discrimination. The Department of Labor was responsible for enforcing the law.

Equality at Work

President Johnson issued Executive Order 11246 on September 24, 1965, which stated in part: "The contractor will not discriminate against any employee or applicant for employment because of race, creed, color, or national origin. The contractor will take affirmative action to ensure that applicants are employed, and that employees are treated during employment, without regard to their race, creed, color, or national origin." [5]

A TIME OF TURMOIL

The decade of the 1960s was a tumultuous time. The Vietnam War was the first war that American citizens

Thurgood Marshall

Thurgood Marshall represented and won more cases before the U.S. Supreme Court than any other American. After *Brown v. Board of Education*, Marshall was appointed to the U.S. Court of Appeals by President John F. Kennedy. In 1965, President Lyndon Johnson appointed Marshall solicitor general. In 1967, Marshall became the first African-American justice in the U.S. Supreme Court. He served as a justice until his retirement in 1991.

did not fully support. President John F. Kennedy and his brother, Robert, were assassinated. Dr. Martin Luther King Jr., the great civil rights leader, and Malcolm X, founder of the Organization of Afro-American Unity, were also assassinated. Changes were taking place in the areas of women's rights and civil rights for minorities.

By the close of the decade, affirmative action would have a positive impact on people who had been discriminated against because of race, religion, sex, age, or disability. But the tumult was not over. For affirmative action, a long and rocky road was still ahead.

President Johnson announces the nomination of Thurgood Marshall to serve on the U.S. Supreme Court.

Arthur Fletcher, chairman of the U.S. Commission on Civil Rights

Labor and Affirmative Action

As of 1967, few minorities were represented in the labor unions. African Americans accounted for fewer than 10 percent of any skilled labor union. The government stepped in to legally attempt to balance the numbers.

The Philadelphia Plan

George Shultz was the Secretary of Labor under President Richard M. Nixon. In 1969, Shultz issued what has come to be known as the Philadelphia Plan. It was based on a similar plan that had been formed during the Johnson administration but never implemented. It was the strongest plan so far to guarantee fair hiring practices in construction jobs. Philadelphia was chosen as a test case. The construction industry in Philadelphia was especially hostile about letting African Americans into their circle, according to Arthur Fletcher, the Assistant Secretary of Labor. Fletcher conceived and implemented the Philadelphia Plan.

On federally funded projects that cost more than $500,000, the Philadelphia Plan required bidders to create a program with specific goals and timetables for improving the representation of minorities in their businesses. In order to win the contract, the bidder did not have to reach the goals, but it had to agree to make a good-faith effort to achieve the goal. The plan set a range of

U.S. Commission on Civil Rights

Arthur Fletcher was an adviser to Presidents Nixon, Ford, Reagan, and George H.W. Bush. He also served as chairman of the U.S. Commission on Civil Rights. He was considered by many to be the father of affirmative action.

percentages for employers to follow in their "good faith" plans.

The Philadelphia Plan was ordered into effect in September 1969. In February 1970, the Department of Labor announced that the Philadelphia Plan would be extended to other cities that did not create their own plans for ending job discrimination in the construction industry.

The Philadelphia Plan set the tone for what followed. The "hometown plans" extended to local contractors, unions, and minority organizations that included private and federal construction contracts. The Office of Federal Contract Compliance Programs (OFCCP) coordinated these as well as other equal opportunity efforts.

Labor unions in Philadelphia were opposed to the plan. They saw these percentages as quotas. They worried that this plan could hurt more qualified workers. One of the requirements of the Civil Rights Act of 1964 had been to prohibit racial

Quota Systems versus Affirmative Action

A quota system requires a defined percentage of minority groups (defined by race or gender) to be admitted to schools or hired and promoted. In this system, a more qualified candidate could be turned down in favor of a minority candidate. The Civil Rights Act of 1964 prohibited racial quotas.

Affirmative action programs work to ensure equality in areas such as school admissions and employment opportunities based on merit regardless of race or gender. The goal is to place diverse groups into higher education and the workplace in approximately the same proportion that they occur in the general population.

*President Lyndon B. Johnson reaches to shake hands
with Dr. Martin Luther King Jr. after signing the Civil Rights Act of 1964
in Washington, D.C., on July 2, 1964.*

quotas. Congress considered legislation to ban the plan
because it was controversial.

The Attorney General supported the Philadelphia
Plan, saying it did not violate the Civil Rights Act
because the setting of goals and timetables with such
mild enforcement did not constitute the setting of
racial quotas. Legislation was passed at all levels of
government, and the Philadelphia Plan was used as a

model. Most government affirmative action plans today that use a mixture of goals and good faith requirements are offshoots of the original Philadelphia Plan.

Challenging the U.S. Government: *Fullilove v. Klutznic*

In 1977, the federal government required that at least 10 percent of all money set aside for federally funded public work contracts be awarded to minority-owned businesses. More than 20 lawsuits were filed claiming that this was unconstitutional and violated the Equal Protection Clause of the Fourteenth Amendment.

The lawsuits also challenged the 10 precent figure. They argued that the number was high considering that African-American contractors only represented 4 percent of the contractors in the United States. The lower federal courts upheld the lawfulness of the program. One of these lawsuits, *Fullilove v. Klutznic,* made it to the U.S. Supreme Court. Fullilove represented contractors and Klutznic was the U.S. Secretary of Congress and represented the government.

The contractors challenged the requirement that 10 percent of the work on federal projects must go to qualified, bona fide minority business owners who also are U.S. citizens. The contractors claimed this was unconstitutional. The Supreme Court denied their claim in 1980. The court stated that reasonable quotas were constitutional.

JOB REQUIREMENTS AND DISCRIMINATION

In December 1970, in *Griggs v. Duke Power Company,* African–American workers at a power plant in North Carolina sued the company. The plant required employees to have a high school education. They also had to pass a standardized intelligence test in order to be eligible for certain jobs. African

Americans were less likely to have a good education. Therefore, the African Americans said that the requirements discriminated against them and did not relate to their ability to perform the jobs.

The plant argued that the requirements were fair and served a solid business purpose. In 1971, the U.S. Supreme Court ruled that the tests and requirements had nothing to do with performing the jobs. This decision made employers—all employers—look carefully at job requirements.

Were the requirements really needed to perform specific jobs, or did they serve to continue discrimination?

Unlawful Barriers

In *Griggs v. Duke Power Company*, decided on March 8, 1971, the court held that employment barriers used to discriminate on the basis of race were unlawful. Testing and measuring procedures could be used only if they provided a reasonable measure of job performance.

Affirmative Action Bypasses Job Seniority

In 1974, the United Steelworkers of America and the Kaiser Aluminum and Chemical Corporation agreed on an affirmative action plan. Prior to 1974, almost all of the advanced jobs (called craftworkers) were held by whites. The companies agreed that 50 percent of all workers selected for in-plant training to become craft-workers would be African American. This would continue until the percentage of African-American craftworkers reflected the percentage of African Americans in the local labor force. The agreement covered 15 Kaiser Aluminum and Chemical Corporation plants.

The first year, the company chose six white and seven African-American craftworker trainees. The most senior of the African Americans had less seniority than many whites who had been waiting for the training. Weber, a white production worker who was not chosen for the training, had seniority over the African Americans. He sued, stating that his civil rights had been violated. The court upheld Kaiser Aluminum and Chemical Corporation's affirmative action plan. The court ruled that on-the-job training given unequally to minorities and Caucasians was legal because the plan was being used to correct an imbalance in the workforce.

Other court cases defined the boundaries of affirmative action as it affected labor pools, jobs, and contracts. The nation's workforce was changing. Most of the workers affected by affirmative action were males.

Steelworkers in the 1970s, part of the changing American workforce

The U.S. Supreme Court has ruled on many important cases involving affirmative action.

UNITED STATES V. PARADISE

Today, most people assume that everyone has an equal opportunity for a job, regardless of race or gender. But historically, this was not always true. Discrimination still exists today. In the early 1970s, many employers, such as the Alabama

Department of Public Safety, did not provide fair opportunities for all people. Phillip Paradise Jr. was one of many people discriminated against by the Alabama Department of Public Safety because of the color of his skin.

Challenging Alabama

In 1972, the NAACP brought action against the Alabama Department of Public Safety. In its 37 years, the Alabama Department of Public Safety had not hired a single African American as a state trooper. The case was labeled *United States v. Paradise.* Phillip Paradise Jr. was named on behalf of a class of African Americans who challenged Alabama. In legal terms, they were the plaintiff.

The U.S. District Court for the Middle District of Alabama ordered the Department of Public Safety to stop discriminating in its hiring practices. The court found that the Alabama Department of Public Safety practiced "pervasive, systematic, and obstinate discriminatory exclusion."[1] In other words, the court ruled that the department had

Plaintiff

The plaintiff is the person or group who brings a lawsuit against the defendant.

purposely excluded blacks from being hired. The court imposed a "one-for-one" hiring quota for the department to follow. Because African Americans made up approximately 25 percent of the available labor pool, the goal was to hire only African Americans until 25 percent of the department was African American.

In Favor: Seeking Equality Beyond Hiring Practices

In 1975, the plaintiffs asked the court for more help. They claimed that the department was hiring very few troopers so that it would not be required to hire African-American troopers. They also claimed the department was not hiring the most qualified African Americans from those seeking jobs. African Americans who were hired were given less than the best training. And African-American troopers received harsher discipline than white troopers for misconduct on the force. As a result, African Americans were leaving the force in greater numbers than whites. The court reaffirmed the 1972 one-for-one hiring order. Yet little changed in the department's hiring practices.

Opposed: Problems with Hiring Practices

In 1977, the plaintiffs returned to court to request

help with the department's promotion practices. The department asked the court to clarify whether the 25 percent order applied only to troopers at the entry level or to all of the higher ranks. The court's response was that the order did not distinguish by rank, and that to:

> … *focus only on the entry-level positions would be to ignore that past discrimination by the department was pervasive, that its effects persist, and that they are manifest. … The order in this case is but the necessary remedy for an intolerable wrong.*[2]

The department argued that more than half of newly hired employees would need to be African American in order to fill the quotas in higher ranks. They also argued that more qualified whites were being passed over in order to fulfill the quotas.

By the end of 1978, the Alabama Department of Public Safety had 232 troopers at the rank of corporal or higher, but not one was an African American. The court approved a partial consent decree in which the department was given one

An Agreement

A consent decree is a court-approved agreement between the plaintiff and defendant.

year to develop a procedure to promote African Americans to its upper ranks. The procedure for promotion had to comply with certain guidelines and be fair to African Americans.

Time to Take Affirmative Steps

The district judge summary in *Paradise v. Prescott*, 1983:

> On February 10, 1984 … twelve years will have passed since this court condemned the racially discriminatory policies and practices of the Alabama Department of Public Safety. Nevertheless, the effects of these policies and practices remain … at all ranks above the entry-level position. Of the 6 majors, there is still not one black. Of the 65 sergeants, there is still not one black. Of the 66 corporals, only four are black. Thus, the department still operates an upper rank structure in which almost every trooper obtained his position through procedures that totally excluded black persons. Moreover, the department is still without acceptable procedures for advancement of black troopers … and it does not appear that any procedures will be in place within the near future. The preceding scenario is intolerable and must not continue. The time has now arrived for the department to take affirmative and substantial steps to open the upper ranks to black troopers.[3]

USING TESTS FOR PROMOTIONS

By April of 1981, the Department of Public Safety still had not promoted any African-American troopers to its upper ranks. More than one year after the deadline, the department finally proposed a selection procedure for promotion. The plaintiff objected to the promotion procedure because it had not proved to be valid or fair.

The court approved a second consent decree in which all troopers seeking promotion to corporal would take a test. The test results would be reviewed to determine whether the test was fair to African Americans under the guidelines that had been set forth. However, the court decided that no promotions would be granted until both parties agreed, or until the court ruled, on the method to be used to decide which troopers were eligible for promotion.

TESTS CAN BE USED UNFAIRLY

The department gave the test to 262 troopers, 60 of whom were African American. Of that 60, only five were listed in the top half of the promotional register. The highest-ranked African American was eightieth from the top of the list. The department declared that it needed to promote eight to ten troopers immediately to the position of corporal. The department planned to use the list to promote those

Civil Rights

The Fourteenth Amendment was ratified on July 9, 1868. It has been referenced many times by both sides in court cases intending to level the playing field for all citizens of the United States: "Section 1: All persons born or naturalized in the United States, and subject to the jurisdiction thereof, are citizens of the United States and of the State wherein they reside. No State shall make or enforce any law which shall abridge the privileges or immunities of citizens of the United States; nor shall any State deprive any person of life, liberty, or property, without due process of law; nor deny to any person within its jurisdiction the equal protection of the laws."[4]

individuals. Further, it planned to use the list to promote 16 to 20 troopers before constructing a new list. Based on the test ranking, no African-American troopers ranked high enough to fill the planned openings.

"It is now years later and this court will not entertain the excuse that the department is now without legal authority to meet its obligations. ... [T]he Department of Personnel, which is also a party to these proceedings, assured the court at the January 5, 1984, hearing that it would work closely with the Public Safety Department to develop acceptable promotion procedures. The Public Safety Department's contention that it is without legal authority is not only meritless, it is frivolous.

"... Such frivolous arguments serve no purpose other than to prolong the discriminatory effects of the department's 37-year history of racial discrimination." [6]

—*District Judge's Conclusion, 1984*

The United States objected to the use of the list to promote troopers. White applicants who had taken the test and ranked from first to seventy-ninth claimed that the one-for-one rule was "unreasonable, illegal, unconstitutional, or against public policy."[5] They objected to promoting African-American troopers in place of white troopers with higher scores. No promotions were made from the list.

SELECTION PROCEDURES

In 1983, the U.S. District Court declared that the department's selection procedure was unfair to African Americans. The department was ordered to submit a new plan to promote at least 15 troopers that was fair to African Americans. The department came back with a proposal to promote four African Americans to corporal out of the 15. The court rejected that proposal. It ordered for a period of time that at least 50 percent of all troopers promoted to corporal and the other upper ranks had to be African American if:

❖ qualified African–American candidates were available.

❖ Less than 25 percent of the rank were African Americans.

❖ the department had not developed a plan to promote African Americans to any given rank that did not negatively affect the rank.

The court gave the department 30 days to submit a schedule to develop fair promotional procedures for all ranks above entry level. The department asked for motions to reconsider the court's decision, stating that it did not have the personnel to design the appropriate promotional procedures. The U.S. District Court denied the motions.

"... the city of Birmingham, the city of Detroit, the city of Los Angeles, and the District of Columbia, state that the operations of police Departments are crippled by the lingering effects of past discrimination. They believe that race-conscious relief in hiring and promotion restores community trust in the fairness of law enforcement and facilitates effective police service by encouraging citizen cooperation."[7]

—*U.S. Supreme Court Justice Brennan*

In February 1984, the department promoted eight African-American troopers and eight non-minority troopers. Four months later, it submitted its proposed promotional procedures. With these procedures in place, the court ruled that the department could promote up to 13 troopers.

Overcoming Past Discrimination

The case was appealed. The U.S. Court of Appeals affirmed the U.S. District Court's order. It said the decision of the court was fair because it was designed to overcome the effects of past discrimination. It was necessary to put the one-for-one hiring and promotion practice in place for a period of time to level the playing field at the Alabama Department of Public Safety.

The case of *Paradise v. Alabama Department of Public Safety* was not unusual. The discrimination seen in the department was not an isolated incident. Many southern states dragged their feet on issues of racial equality. Strong tools such as affirmative action were needed.

"[I]n a city with a recent history of racial unrest, the superintendent of police might reasonably conclude that an integrated police force could develop a better relationship with the community and do a more effective job of maintaining law and order than a force composed only of white officers."[8]

—U.S. Supreme Court Justice Brennan

Gavel of justice

Chapter

6

Susan B. Anthony and Elizabeth Cady Stanton were two nineteenth-century women deeply involved in gaining the vote for American women.

WOMEN AND AFFIRMATIVE ACTION

Women have not always had the freedom to become what they want, go where they want, own property, vote, or compete in athletics. The rights of women changed drastically during the twentieth century.

The women's movement had its roots with Susan B. Anthony, Elizabeth Cady Stanton, Lucretia Mott, and their colleagues. In July 1848, the first convention for women's rights was held in Seneca Falls, New York. More than 70 years later, in 1920, women finally won the right to vote.

However, there was still much ground to be covered before women were considered equal to men. There was still a large equality gap between women and men. Women were becoming a presence in the workforce—mostly as teachers, nurses, store clerks, and secretaries. These jobs were deemed appropriate for women.

Education

Title IX was the first federal law that made it illegal to discriminate against students (and employees of schools) on the basis of gender.

The Title IX Education Amendments of 1972 included: "… No person in the United States shall, on the basis of sex, be excluded from participation in, be denied the benefits of, or be subjected to discrimination under any education program or activity receiving Federal financial assistance. … [A]n educational institution means any public or private preschool, elementary, or secondary school, or any institution of vocational, professional, or higher education. …"[1]

In 1933, during the Great Depression, the National Recovery Act was passed. In an effort to boost the economy, the act forbid more than one person in a family from working at a wage-earning job. Since men generally earned higher wages, many married women lost their jobs.

Equal Pay

In 1938, the Fair Labor Standards Act established a minimum wage, regardless of gender. However, the act only applied to the minimum wage. Not until 1963, when Congress passed the Equal Pay Act, did legislation address equal pay regardless of race, color, religion, national origin, or sex of the worker. In 1964, the Civil Rights Act prohibited discrimination in employment based on race, color, religion, national origin, or sex.

Family

Many cases have been brought to court regarding employment of women who are parents or about to become parents. One such case was *Phillips v. Martin Marietta Corporation* (1971). The U.S. Supreme Court ruled that it was not legal for private employers to discriminate against women by refusing to hire women who were the mothers of preschoolers. In 1978, the Pregnancy Discrimination Act banned employment discrimination against women who were pregnant or who had a pregnancy-related condition.

In 1993, the Family and Medical Leave Act (FMLA) went into effect. It grants up to 12 weeks of unpaid leave for the birth and care of the employee's newborn

Roberta White used unpaid time off work through the Family and Medical Leave Act to care for her father, who has battled lung cancer, diabetes, and heart disease.

or adopted child, to take medical leave for a serious health issue, or to take care of a parent, spouse, or child with a serious health issue.

EDUCATION AND ATHLETICS

By the 1960s, women's rights were becoming more fully established. Affirmative action played a major part in helping women gain equality in education and athletics as well as the workplace.

One of the most important legal documents for women has been Title IX of the Education Amendments. Title IX prohibits discrimination based on gender in federally funded education or activities. President Richard M. Nixon signed Title IX into law in June 1972.

Recognition of Women

The following excerpts are from the Declaration of Sentiments which demanded the recognition of women and the same rights as men.

We hold these truths to be self-evident: that all men and women are created equal …

The history of mankind is a history of repeated injuries …

He has compelled her to submit to laws, in the formation of which she had no voice …

He has taken from her all right in property, even to the wages she earns …

He has denied her the facilities for obtaining a thorough education, all colleges being closed against her.

… in view of the unjust laws above mentioned, and because women do feel themselves aggrieved, oppressed, and fraudulently deprived of their most sacred rights, we insist that they have immediate admission to all the rights and privileges which belong to them as citizens of the United States.[2]

Title IX has become known as the law that allows girls to play athletics, but its purpose is broader than that. Title IX has helped women become doctors, lawyers, mechanics, and members of many other professions that had been dominated by men. Title IX applies to traditional educational institutions and to any education or training program receiving federal financial assistance.

In 1997, the U.S. Supreme Court revisited Title IX. The court ruled that college athletics programs must involve approximately the same numbers of men and women in various sports to qualify for federal funding.

Title IX has changed the face of school sports. In 1971, fewer than 300,000 girls participated in interscholastic sports. By 1997, more than 2.4 million girls were playing in interscholastic sports.

In the past, talented athletes such as Sheryl Swoopes might have gone unnoticed. Born in 1971, Swoopes played basketball for Texas Tech. She won three Olympic gold medals. She became a star in the Women's National Basketball Association (WNBA). She was the top scorer in the 2005 season and a member of the 2006 USA Basketball Women's World Championship team. Thanks to Title IX, Swoopes and others have had opportunities to excel.

The Glass Ceiling

Women are less likely to be promoted to the top positions in large or major businesses. This invisible barrier to advancement is called a glass ceiling. A March 1995 Federal Glass Ceiling Commission report determined that approximately:

- 97 percent of the senior managers in Fortune 1000 industrial companies and Fortune 500 companies are men.

- 48 percent of all journalists are women, but they account for only 6 percent of the top jobs.

- 23 percent of lawyers are women, but they account for only 11 percent of the law firm partners.

Room for Improvement

The opportunities for women in sports have increased, and women now earn almost half of all bachelors and masters degrees. However, women earn only one-third of all doctorate degrees. Fewer women than men receive any level of degree in the fields of math, engineering, and physical sciences. In the workforce, women are less likely to be promoted to senior management and executive positions. ⁓

Athletics

Cheryl Miller was an outstanding member of the 1984 Olympic gold medal women's basketball team. She states that, "Without Title IX, I'd be nowhere."[3]

Sheryl Swoopes is among the original WNBA All-Stars.

Crowds in front of the Lincoln Memorial during the March on Washington for Civil Rights on August 28, 1963

MINORITY POPULATIONS

The wording on most documents that relates to affirmative action describes people who have been discriminated against because of race, color, religion, national origin, gender, age, or disability. When affirmative action first became a buzzword, most

people immediately thought of African Americans. After all, affirmative action followed the Civil Rights Act, which suppressed the Jim Crow laws.

The term "minority" in regard to race means many things. In general, it applies to someone who is not Caucasian. For example, a person could be all or part African American, Asian American, or Native American and be considered a minority. In the 2000 census, many Native Americans and approximately 2 million African Americans considered themselves to be multi-racial. Approximately 25 percent of African-American white people, 50 percent of Asian-American white people, and 80 percent of Native American white people all considered themselves white. It is becoming more difficult to use race as a factor in determining who qualifies to be a recipient of affirmative action.

WOMEN

Affirmative action does not only apply to race. Women were not being openly discriminated against in the same way as African Americans and other minorities. For example, white women did not have to use separate restaurants and water fountains or sit in the back of the bus. Discrimination against women was more subtle—but it was real. Until quite recently, women did not have

the same opportunities in education and options
for careers and advancement as men. The women's
movement and "women's liberation" followed, to a great
extent, the same timeline as the Civil Rights Movement.
However, it could be argued that women are not a
minority, but rather the majority. In the general
population, slightly more than half of the people are
female.

Other Minorities

Affirmative action has endeavored to help people,
including those who:

❖ Practice religions other than Christianity.

❖ Immigrated to the United States and became
citizens.

❖ Are physically and mentally disabled.

❖ Practice different sets of beliefs or lifestyles.

❖ Served in the armed forces.

Affirmative action is charged with placing diverse
populations into higher education and the workplace
in roughly the same proportion that they occur
in the general public. Assume 75 percent of a city's
population consists of Asian-born Americans.
Now assume that only 3 percent are in college and only

Supporters of the Equal Rights Amendment on August 26, 1977, following President Jimmy Carter's signing of a Women's Equality Day proclamation

5 percent are in the local workforce. Affirmative action support might be needed to place more Asian Americans into higher education and the local workforce.

Disabilities

In 1973, President Richard M. Nixon signed into law Section 503 of the Vocational Rehabilitation Act. This law requires employers with federal contracts or subcontracts of more than $10,000 to take affirmative action in hiring, retaining, and promoting qualified employees who have physical or mental disabilities. It prohibits colleges and universities from discriminating against students with disabilities.

The Americans with Disabilities Act (ADA) of 1990 prohibits discrimination against anyone with disabilities. This includes the areas of employment, transportation, public accommodations, communications, and governmental activities. The ADA also requires reasonable accommodation of an individual's

Fulfilling America's Promise to Americans With Disabilities

Disability will touch most Americans at some point during their lives. Over 54 million Americans have disabilities. In addition, more than 25 million family members are caregivers. Millions more provide aid and assistance to people with disabilities.

In 1990, President George H.W. Bush signed the Americans with Disabilities Act (ADA). This is one of the most significant civil rights laws since the Civil Rights Act of 1964.

In 1999, Congress passed the Ticket-to-Work and Work Incentives Improvement Act.

More than 7.5 million Americans with disabilities receive benefits under federal disability programs. However, in part because of disincentives in federal law, fewer than 1 percent of those receiving disability benefits are able to enter the workforce.

Prior to the Ticket-to-Work law, in order to continue to receive disability payments and health coverage, recipients could not engage in any substantial work. The Ticket-to-Work law provides incentives for people with disabilities to return to work.

disability. The Individuals with Disabilities Education Act (IDEA) ensures that all children with disabilities receive a free public education. Children with disabilities are entitled to services and equipment that make education accessible to them. This includes speech therapy, occupational therapy, physical therapy, special transportation, or special equipment such as computers and physical adaptive devices.

The Civil Rights Act of 1991 amended the 1964 Civil Rights Act by adding a category labeled "disability." The 1991 act also provided solutions for dealing with discrimination against people with disabilities.

> "Under Section 503 and its implementing regulations, an 'individual with a disability' means a person who (1) has a physical or mental impairment that substantially limits one or more major life activities, (2) has a record of such impairment, or (3) is regarded as having such an impairment.
>
> "A 'qualified individual with a disability' means a person with a disability who satisfies the job-related requirements of the employment position he or she holds or is applying for, and who, with or without reasonable accommodation, can perform the essential job functions of that position."[1]
>
> —*Rehabilitation Act of 1973*

Vietnam Veterans

Section 402 of the Veterans Readjustment Act of 1974 requires that federal contractors take affirmative action to employ qualified disabled veterans and

Questions a Prospective Employer Cannot Ask

- Where were you born?
- How old are you?
- What year were you born?
- When did you graduate from high school?
- Are you married?
- Is this your maiden or married name?
- Do you have children?
- Do you plan to have children?
- Are you pregnant?
- What's your heritage?
- What race are you?
- Are you a member of a minority group?
- What religion are you?
- Have you ever been arrested?
- Have you ever spent a night in jail?
- Do you have any disabilities?

veterans of the Vietnam War. The act prohibits discrimination based on a veteran's status as a Vietnam-era vet or on an otherwise qualified veteran's disability.

Privacy

Sometimes employers do not know and should not be able to find out certain things about a person. This includes whether the job applicant is married. Employers also cannot ask what religion a job candidate practices or how a person lives. Not asking such questions is a result of legislation that is related to affirmative action.

Pat Blevins of Lake Preston, South Dakota, stands near a parade to honor veterans of the Vietnam War. The parade and dedication of a memorial help Vietnam veterans feel welcome after facing disrespect when they returned nearly four decades ago.

Affirmative action rulings have impacted the makeup of college campuses.

HIGHER EDUCATION AND THE U.S. SUPREME COURT

ffirmative action was being put to work in the labor force. However, college and university administrators realized in order for society to change, the makeup of the student body needed to change.

The change has been slow in coming. As of 1955, African Americans accounted for 4.9 percent of all college students between the ages of 18 and 24. The figure rose slightly during the next few years, but the percentage had slumped to 4.9 again by 1965. After affirmative action measures were introduced, the national averages began to reflect a change in the student body.

- ❖ By 1970, 7.8 percent were African American.

- ❖ By 1980, 9.1 percent were African American.

- ❖ By 1990, 11.3 percent were African American.

UNIVERSITY OF CALIFORNIA V. BAKKE

Many universities actively recruited minorities. They rewrote their admissions criteria to enable more minorities to qualify for admission. It became easier for minorities to receive financial aid and scholarships. Universities were reaping the benefits

Prohibiting Discrimination

Title VI was enacted as part of the landmark Civil Rights Act of 1964. It prohibits discrimination on the basis of race, color, and national origin in programs and activities receiving federal financial assistance. As President John F. Kennedy stated in 1963:

"Simple justice requires that public funds, to which all taxpayers of all races [colors, and national origins] contribute, not be spent in any fashion which encourages, entrenches, subsidizes or results in racial [color or national origin] discrimination."[1]

of a diverse student population. However, was diversity always a good thing? Were standards lowered in order to allow more diverse students onto the college campus? Were white students, especially white male students, experiencing reverse discrimination?

Allan Bakke, a white student, thought so. In 1973 and again in 1974, Bakke applied to the University of California, Davis, Medical School. The school had reserved 16 of the 100 slots in its entering class for minority students. Even though Bakke's test scores and grades were higher than what was expected of minority students, he was denied entrance into the school both years. He sued. In 1977, his case reached the U.S. Supreme Court.

The University of California Medical School reasoned that the quota program would:

❖ Reduce the "historic deficit" of minorities.

❖ Counter the effects of discrimination on society.

❖ Increase the number of doctors who were willing to work in communities that were underserved.

❖ Provide educational benefits that a diverse student population can bring.

Four of the nine U.S. Supreme Court justices (led by Justice Stevens) ruled in favor of Bakke. They voted that he should be admitted to the medical school. They used the wording from Title VI of the Civil Rights Act to support this decision.

Four other justices (led by Justice Brennan) wanted to save the medical school's program. They said that Title VI had no independent meaning. Instead, they looked at the U.S. Constitution—specifically the Fourteenth Amendment. They interpreted the amendment as favorable to the minority students.

That left one justice—and he had yet a different perspective. Justice Powell found the first three of the university's reasons to be insufficient for not accepting Bakke. Justice Powell did agree with the idea of providing a diverse population for the school. However, he did not agree that the special set-aside program was necessary to achieve the desired results. Although Justice Powell agreed with Justice Brennan's group's interpretation that Title VI was not strong enough, he did not agree with their interpretation of the Fourteenth Amendment. Justice Powell simply stated that the medical school's policy was unconstitutional. He ruled in favor with Justice Stevens' group. Five out of the nine justices supported Allen Bakke.

The ruling came down on June 28, 1978, in the case of the *University of California v. Bakke.* The U.S. Supreme Court ruled that universities might consider that minority status can be used as a factor in admissions, but quotas (such as the University of California Medical School's setting aside 16 out of 100 slots) were unconstitutional.

Not everyone agreed with the U.S. Supreme Court's decision.

HOPWOOD V. TEXAS

In 1992, Cheryl Hopwood and three white male law school applicants challenged the University of Texas's affirmative action program. The four said that they were overlooked in favor of less qualified minority students. In 1996, the Fifth U.S. Court of Appeals stated that the *Bakke* decision, in which quotas were not allowed but race could serve as a factor in admissions, was invalid. The court suspended the University of Texas's affirmative action admissions program.

The court rejected educational diversity as a legitimate goal for a college campus. In 1997, the Attorney General of Texas announced that all public Texas institutions of higher learning should use race-neutral criteria. With the race-neutral criteria in place,

Allan Bakke attends his first day at the University of California at Davis on September 25, 1978. Bakke sued the university for reverse discrimination.

admissions in the following year dropped 64 percent for Latinos and 88 percent for African Americans.

Gratz v. Bollinger

In 1995, Jennifer Gratz applied to the University of Michigan's College of Literature, Science, and the Arts (LSA). She did not gain admission to the college. In 1997, Patrick Hamacher applied and also was denied admission as a transfer student. Both well-qualified candidates were white. In 1997, they filed a lawsuit in the U.S. District Court (Detroit) against the University of Michigan. Eventually both plaintiffs entered other universities.

Michigan's LSA used a formula for admitting new students in which all candidates who were from "an underrepresented minority group" were awarded an extra 20 points. Points were also awarded based on high school grades, standardized test scores, geography, leadership ability, curriculum strength (such as athletic

---

Opinion of the Court from *Gratz v. Bollinger*

Also instructive in our consideration of the LSA's system is the example provided in the description of the Harvard College Admissions Program. ... The example was included to 'illustrate the kind of significance attached to race' under the Harvard College program. ... It provided as follows:

'The admissions Committee, with only a few places left to fill, might find itself forced to choose between A, the child of a successful black physician in an academic community with promise of superior academic performance, and B, a black ... whose academic achievement was lower but who had demonstrated energy and leadership as well as an apparently abiding interest in black power. If a good number of black students much like A but few like B had already been admitted, the Committee might prefer B; and vice versa. If C, a white student with extraordinary artistic talent, were also seeking one of the remaining places, his unique quality might give him an edge over both A and B. Thus, the critical criteria are often individual qualities or experience not dependent upon race but sometimes associated with it.'[2]

ability, musical ability, artistic talent, etc.), and alumni relations. Students needed 100 points for admission.

In 2000, in *Gratz v. Bollinger*, the U.S. District Court confirmed that public universities may use affirmative action to ensure a diverse student body. The court said that the use of race as a factor in admissions was constitutional. The court further stated that the use of race as a factor was similar to granting preference to children of alumni or to athletes. The court stated that an affirmative action program that allows for a diverse student body provides educational benefits. The case eventually reached the U.S. Supreme Court. On June 23, 2003, the U.S. Supreme Court ruled that LSA's formulaic point system to rate potential students had to be modified.

Achieving Diversity

Statement by the National Security Advisor, Dr. Condoleezza Rice, January 17, 2003:

"… the President … asked for my view on how diversity can be best achieved on university campuses. I offered my view, drawing on my experience in academia and as provost of a major university. I agree with the President's position, which emphasizes the need for diversity and recognizes the continued legacy of racial prejudice, and the need to fight it. The President challenged universities to develop ways to diversify their populations fully. I believe that while race neutral means are preferable, it is appropriate to use race as one factor among others in achieving a diverse student body."[3]

Grutter v. Bollinger

Also in 1997, three anti-affirmative action groups filed a lawsuit on behalf of Barbara Grutter and other white applicants (41 total) against the University of Michigan Law School. This suit was named *Grutter v. Bollinger*. The law school's admission policy was based on a student's academic ability and a flexible assessment of their talents, experiences, and potential. Decisions were made on the basis of the material in a student's file. This included a personal statement, letters of recommendation, and an essay by the applicant about how they would contribute to school life and diversity. It also included the applicant's grade-point average and law school admissions test score.

Grutter contended that race was a predominant factor in denying her admission to the law school. The judge drew a different conclusion, in that intellectual diversity is not the same as racial diversity. The U.S. District Court found that the use of race as a factor in its admissions decisions was unconstitutional and in violation of Title VI or the 1964 Civil Rights Act. In 2002, the U.S. Court of Appeals reversed the decision. The case went to the U.S. Supreme Court.

On January 15, 2003, President George W. Bush put forth the following message regarding the Michigan affirmative action case:

> *The Supreme Court will soon hear arguments in a case about admission policies and student diversity in public universities. I strongly support diversity of all kinds, including racial diversity in higher education. But the method used by the University of Michigan to achieve this important goal is fundamentally flawed.*

> *... the Michigan policies amount to a quota system that unfairly rewards or penalizes perspective students, based solely on their race ... and establishes numerical targets for incoming minority students, are unconstitutional.*

> *Our Constitution makes it clear that people of all races must be treated equally under the law. Yet we know that our society has not fully achieved that ideal. Racial prejudice is a reality in America. ... Yet, as we work to address the wrong of racial prejudice, we must not use means that create another wrong, and thus perpetuate our divisions.*

> *America is a diverse country, racially, economically, and ethnically. And our institutions of higher education should reflect our diversity. ... Yet quota systems that use race to include or exclude people from higher education and the opportunities it offers are divisive, unfair and impossible to square with the Constitution.[4]*

Japanese students at the University of Northern Michigan's campus

A ruling was made on June 23, 2003, to uphold the University of Michigan Law School's "individualized consideration" policy. And, it ruled that race can be one of many factors that a school considers when selecting students in order to obtain a diverse student body. The *Gratz* and *Grutter* cases gained a lot of national attention. These cases renewed the public's interest in affirmative action. Everyone—including President

Bush—had a differing opinion regarding the Court's decision.

University Diversity Statistics

Many court cases involve university admissions policies. Lawsuits have been brought by minorities and by whites. These cases serve as an example of the kind of careful consideration institutions of higher education in the United States have had to deal with while forming their affirmative action policies.

Today, almost any university Web site shows information about its affirmative action policy or statistics that show the diversity of the university. The University of Texas at Austin reports that in 2005, 50.9 percent of the students were female and 49.1 percent were male students.

The breakdown of races/ethnicities is given as:

❖ 57.4 percent White.

❖ 14.3 percent Asian American.

❖ 14.1 percent Hispanic.

❖ 3.7 percent African American.

Opinion of the Court in *Grutter v. Bollinger:*

"The Law School's claim is further bolstered by numerous expert studies and reports showing that such diversity promotes learning outcomes and better prepares students for an increasingly diverse workforce, for society, and for the legal profession."[5]

❖ 0.4 percent American Indian.

❖ 10 percent foreign and unknown.

The University of Michigan Web site includes a 2002 study that shows percentages of the student body by "students of color." This includes Asian-Pacific Americans. African Americans, Latino/Hispanics, and Native Americans. The study gave the following statistics:

❖ In 1981, the total was 9.4 percent.

❖ In 1987, the total was 13.6 percent.

❖ In 1991, the total was 20.5 percent.

❖ In 2001, the total was 26.1 percent.

Allan Bakke talks with a fellow graduates at the Medical School of the University of California, Davis, on Friday, June 4, 1982.

Affirmative action supporters cheer speakers on the steps of the Capitol in Olympia, Washington, on January 27, 1998.

AFFIRMATIVE ACTION
EXPERIENCES

Many people have benefited from the federal affirmative action plans. The Department of Labor follows some of these success stories. By monitoring affirmative action, lawmakers hope to better understand how is affects society.

In Favor: Affirmative Action Assists the Underpriviledged

Bernadette is an African-American single parent with two children. She lives in Washington, D.C. Thanks to a federal affirmative action program, she works as a carpenter. This enables her to make a good wage to support her family and give her children some of the social and educational benefits that a higher salary can provide.

Janice has been an astronaut with NASA at the Johnson Space Center. Since July 1991, she has logged more than 438 hours in space. Janice states:

> *Under NASA's developing equal opportunity and diversity policies, all hiring and advancement decisions are based on individual qualifications and merit, but recruitment and development programs are structured such that high-quality candidates are available to help achieve a representative workforce.*[1]

"From the experience of southern blacks, a generation of Americans came to realize with new force that there are forms of oppression that touch all levels of a society. This was the crucial lesson that survived the turbulence in the South of the fifties and sixties. The southern movement gave impetus initially to the civil rights drives of nonwhite Americans in the North. Later, the black movement's vitality extended to animate the liberation movements of women, the elderly, the physically disabled, and the homosexual. Leaders of these groups described the oppression they suffered by analogy to that suffered by blacks."[2]

—Richard Rodriguez, author on, and beneficiary of, affirmative action

Judy is a single parent. She lives in Chicago, Illinois, with two teenaged sons. To make ends meet, she worked two jobs and had no chance for advancement. Today, she is a structural ironworker. She believes she would not have this job without affirmative action. Judy was one of only 20 women in her union of more than 2,300 members.

Lisa worked in Hammond, Indiana, as a seamstress without benefits for $5 an hour. She now earns more than $20 an hour with benefits. Lisa credits affirmative action for her success.

In their book, *The Shape of the River: Long-Term Consequences of Considering Race in College and University Admissions*, William G. Bowen and Derek Bok argue in favor of affirmative action. They state that African-American and Hispanic students who have advanced degrees are the "backbone" of the new middle-class culture of African Americans and Hispanics. Successful professionals serve as role models for younger generations. Bowen and Bok argue that minority people who are successful professionals are changing the society.

Bowen and Bok conducted an extensive study of white and African-American students at 28 colleges. The study found that African-American graduates were more likely to be involved in community activities than their white classmates. The study also found that both African-American and white students felt that they enjoyed a great deal of interaction with other races during their college years. Bowen and Bok conclude that affirmative action policies have helped diverse populations live and work together and that the policies have helped minority populations better themselves in the world.

Opposed: Some Minorities Do Not Require Assistance

There is another viewpoint. Richard Rodriguez is the son of Mexican immigrants who, although they did not speak much English, provided their children a comfortable, middle-class life. His parents settled in a white neighborhood in Sacramento, California, rather than in the Mexican section of town. His father worked; his mother stayed home to take care of the family.

When Rodriguez began school, he spoke only a few words of English. He learned English, which he considered the public language of the United States. Spanish was his private, family language. Rodriguez always did quite well in school. He calls himself a "scholarship boy," explaining that he was anxious and eager to learn. He read and studied all the time. When a question was asked in class, his hand would shoot up. He had the answer. He wanted to excel. Later, he realized that he had not been thinking for himself. He had not been making his learning his own. Rather, he had been reciting back what his teachers wanted to hear.

On Affirmative Action
by Scott W. Williams

Is there enough racism to warrant affirmative action? 'No longer!' is what I hear from contemporary whites. To them, history is forgotten or irrelevant. For me it is different, my mother's 1937 University of Maine master's degree in mathematics was not good enough for Ph.D. work at other institutions and was only fit for high school teaching … my father's Penn State Ph.D. in Experimental Psychology … was only good enough for work as a Coast Guard cook in World War II, and for 15 to 24 hour/week teaching positions in Black colleges the next 35 years.

… Prior to 1965, it was virtually impossible for a black to get a faculty position at a non-black institution no matter whether degrees came from Harvard or the University of Michigan. Too many faculty members shared the general public's overt racism.[3]

Rodriguez progressed through school, enjoying the attention that doing well in academics brought him. He attended Stanford University. In his book, *Hunger of Memory*, he says that Stanford attracted him because of its academic reputation and also because it was a school of upper-middle-class whites. He went on to graduate school at

Columbia and Berkeley as a minority student. During college, partly thanks to a summer job working construction, he became proud of his brown skin. He mentions walking on campus and seeing white students lying in the sun, working on their tans.

In the mid- and late-1960s, the Civil Rights Movement was in full swing. Non-whites became more vocal about equal opportunity and higher education for all. Rodriguez was rewarded for his eagerness to learn. His Spanish last name and dark skin were an asset. He got into the schools he wanted. He applied for, and received, fellowships and study grants. When he needed a teaching assistantship, he got it. When he graduated and began looking for a university teaching position, he had no trouble being accepted anywhere he wanted to go. In fact, because he was part of an under-represented minority, prestigious colleges came looking for him.

"In the late 1960s non-white Americans clamored for access to higher education, and I became a principal beneficiary of the academy's response, its programs of affirmative action. My presence was noted each fall by the campus press office in its proud tally of Hispanic–American students enrolled; my progress was followed by HEW statisticians. One of the lucky ones. Rewarded. Advanced for belonging to a racial group 'under-represented' in American institutional life."[4]

—*Richard Rodriguez*

As the 1970s began, Rodriguez became disillusioned with the term "minority." He gave up the idea of being a college professor. Classmates who were just as bright as he was, but who were born with white skin, did not have an easy time finding professorships. Rodriguez knew that he was wanted on many campuses, not because he was better than his classmates, but because he was a minority. Instead of teaching, he decided to write.

In 1974, Rodriguez wrote an essay that was published. He wrote of being uneasy as a beneficiary of affirmative action. He wrote more articles against affirmative action. Rodriguez stated that he had not been a disadvantaged minority and that he had received unfair advantages over others. Even his essay against affirmative action won him praise and a kind of celebrity. Before long, he began receiving hate mail from activists. One such letter called him the white people's "fawning pet."[5] Other people—especially white people—seemed to think that, because Rodriguez was Mexican-American, he deserved the advantages he had received.

Members of a loosely-knit coalition of white male University of California, Berkeley, students calling for increased campus diversity

President Bill Clinton

YESTERDAY, TODAY, AND TOMORROW

The term "affirmative action" came into use in the 1960s. Since that time, many changes have occurred in society. The concept of affirmative action began approximately at the same time as forced integration. Job discrimination against women, minorities, and others has been recognized and challenged. Enrollment policies of schools, from preschools through universities, have been challenged. Most schools are no longer segregated. Due to affirmative action, people of all colors, national origins, genders, and abilities have been given a step up. The fight continues.

LEGISLATION, STATE INITIATIVES, AND U.S. SUPREME COURT RULINGS

On November 21, 1991, President George H.W. Bush signed the Civil Rights Act of 1991. This new Civil Rights Act strengthened the existing civil rights laws. It also provided a means for damages in cases of intentional discrimination in employment.

In 1995, President Bill Clinton addressed affirmative action in a speech titled, "Mend It, Don't End It." His point was that inequities still

Excerpt from President Clinton's 1995 "Mend It, Don't End It" Speech

"Justice Thurgood Marshall, the grandson of a slave, said, 'The government our founders devised was defective from the start, requiring several amendments, a civil war, and momentous social transformation to attain the system of constitutional government and its respect for the individual freedoms and human rights we hold as fundamental today.'

"Emancipation, women's suffrage, civil rights, voting rights, equal rights, the struggle for the rights of the disabled—all these and other struggles are milestones on America's often rocky but fundamentally righteous journey to close the gap between the ideals enshrined in these treasures here in the National Archives and the reality of our daily lives."[1]

exist in U.S. society, and that affirmative action is still needed, even though it is imperfect. On the same day of the speech, he issued a White House Memorandum calling for the elimination of any program that:

❖ creates a quota

❖ creates preferences for unqualified individuals

❖ creates reverse discrimination

❖ continues after it has fulfilled its goal.

Ban on Affirmative Action

Mary Sue Coleman, president of the University of Michigan, in a speech to students the day after Michigan voters approved a ban on affirmative action:

"Diversity matters at Michigan, today more than any day in our history.

"It matters today, and it will matter tomorrow. It will always matter because it is what makes us the great university we are.

"I am deeply disappointed that the voters of our state have rejected affirmative action as a way to help build a community that is fair and equal for all.

"But we will not be deterred in the all-important work of creating a diverse, welcoming campus. We will not be deterred."[2]

On November 3, 1997, the citizens of California voted on Proposition 209. The goal of this initiative was to place a state ban on all forms of affirmative action. Under proposition 209, public college admissions and public employers would not be required to consider affirmative action regarding ethnic origin, gender, or race. Proposition 209 was approved by the voters. One year later, in December of 1998, citizens in the state of Washington voted for a similar ban on affirmative action.

University of California v. Bakke

This case ruled that minority status can be used as a factor in determining school admissions, but quotas are unconstitutional.

The U.S. Supreme Court decision on June 23, 2003 ruled that race can be one of many factors that a school considers when selecting students in order to obtain a diverse student body. The ruling by the U.S. Supreme Court has been called the most important affirmative action decision since the *University of California v. Bakke* in 1978.

In November of 2006, the citizens of Michigan voted on the Michigan Civil Rights Initiative (MCRI) proposal to ban affirmative action. Jennifer Gratz, who had brought the under-graduate lawsuit against the University of Michigan in 1995, served as the executive director of the MCRI. She and others who pushed for the ban on affirmative action said that the MCRI proposal would end racial preferences. This initiative, called Proposal 2, passed by a 58–to–42 percent margin (approximately 1.8 million votes for it and 1.3 million votes against it).

"The unemployment rate for African Americans remains twice that of whites. The Hispanic rate is still higher. Women have narrowed the earnings gap, but they still make only 72% as much as men do for comparable jobs. The average income for a Hispanic woman with a college degree is still less than the average income of a white man with a high school diploma. … White men make up 43% of our workforce, but they hold 95% of these jobs."[3]

The *Coalition to Defend Affirmative Action, Integration, and Immigration Rights By Any Means Necessary* (BAMN) is a pro-affirmative action group. The group brought a lawsuit to challenge Proposal 2, which the Michigan voters had passed in 2006.

On June 28, 2007, the U.S. Supreme Court ruled against the assigning of students to individual public schools on the basis of race. Chief Justice Robert's statement to the court was that using a person's race explicitly furthers discrimination. Opponents to the Court's decision worry that it will lead to the resegregation of public schools.

AFFIRMATIVE ACTION'S FUTURE

Although affirmative action has been challenged and redefined, it is still alive. What is its future? Two things are certain: the debate will continue, and the United States will continue to find tools to level the playing field so that all people will one day be able to live up to their true potential.

NASA astronaut Stephanie Wilson speaks to students at Taconic High School in Pittsfield, Massachusetts, during a visit to her hometown on September 12, 2006. Wilson was the second African-American woman in space.

TIMELINE

1791

The U.S. Constitution and Bill of Rights legitimize slavery.

1865

Thirteenth Amendment abolishes slavery. Southern states create codes to segregate blacks.

1866

The Civil Rights Act invalidates the codes.

1896

U.S. Supreme Court holds that "separate but equal" accommodations are constitutional.

1920

The Nineteenth Amendment gives women the right to vote, August 18.

1954

Legal school segregation is ended and desegregation begins on May 17.

1868

Fourteenth Amendment grants citizenship to everyone born in the United States.

1870

Fifteenth Amendment gives freedmen the right to vote.

1875

Civil Rights Act guarantees men equal access to public accommodations regardless of race or color.

1961

On March 6, Executive Order 10925 prohibits discrimination in federal government hiring.

1964

On July 2, the Civil Rights Act seeks to end discrimination by private companies with 15 or more employees.

1965

In September, Executive Order 11246 requires federal contractors to take affirmative action to ensure equality of employment.

TIMELINE

1967	1969	1972
Executive Order 11246 is amended to include women.	Philadelphia Plan sets goals for the construction trades to achieve equal opportunity in employment.	Title IX prohibits discrimination against girls and women in federally funded education and athletic programs.

1978	1997	1998
U.S. Supreme Court rules on June 28 that universities may consider minority status as a factor in admissions, but quotas are unconstitutional.	On November 3, California residents vote to ban affirmative action.	In December, Washington residents vote for a similar ban on affirmative action.

1972

Businesses receiving government funds must purchase some goods and services from minority and women-owned businesses.

1973

Federal contractors cannot discriminate on the basis of physical or mental handicaps.

1974

The Veterans Readjustment Act requires federal contractors to take affirmative action in employing disabled veterans.

2003

U.S. Supreme Court confirms public universities may use affirmative action to ensure a diverse student body.

2006

Michigan residents vote to ban affirmative action.

2007

On June 28, the U.S. Supreme Court rules against assigning students to public schools on the basis of race.

ESSENTIAL FACTS

AT ISSUE

Opposed

Affirmative action is no longer necessary.
Hiring and admissions decisions should be based on merit.
Affirmative action bypasses job seniority.
Using tests eliminates personal bias.

In Favor

Minorities are underrepresented.
Tests are biased.
Minorities are at a disadvantage compared to counterparts.
Affirmative action corrects a historical imbalance.

CRITICAL DATES

1954
The U.S. Supreme Court decision in *Brown v. Board of Education* marked the end of school segregation and the beginning of integration.

1964
Segregation in public schools is unconstitutional. The Civil Rights Act of 1964 banned discrimination in education and employment on the basis of race and gender (and was later amended to include disabilities).

1964
Congress passed the Equal Employment Opportunity Act and the Equal Opportunity Act.

1972
Title IX of the Education Amendments Act prohibited discrimination against girls and women in federally funded education. This included athletic programs.

1972, 1975, 1987
In decisions from the late 1970s and early 1980s, *United States v. Paradise* required the Alabama Department of Public Safety hire equal numbers of African Americans and whites for positions as troopers.

1978
In the decision of *University of California v. Bakke*, the U.S. Supreme Court ruled that minority status can be a factor in admissions, but quotas in higher education were unconstitutional.

June 23, 2003
The U.S. Supreme Court decision ruled that race can be one of many factors that a school considers when selecting students in order to obtain a diverse student body.

Quotes

Opposed

"… the Michigan policies amount to a quota system that unfairly rewards or penalizes prospective students, based solely on their race … and establishes numerical targets for incoming minority students, are unconstitutional."—*President George W. Bush*

In Favor

"Is there enough racism to warrant affirmative action? 'No longer!' is what I hear from contemporary whites. To them, history is forgotten or irrelevant. For me it is different."—*Scott W. Williams, author*

ADDITIONAL RESOURCES

SELECT BIBLIOGRAPHY

Bergmann, Barbara R. *In Defense of Affirmative Action*. New York: BasicBooks, 1996.

Bok, Derek and Bowen, William G. *The Shape of the River: Long-Term Consequences of Considering Race in College and University Admissions*. Princeton: Princeton University Press, 1998.

Cose, Ellis. *Color-Blind (Seeing Beyond Race in a Race-Obsessed World)*. New York: HarperCollins, 1997.

Kotz, Nick. *Judgment Days: Lyndon Baines Johnson, Martin Luther King Jr., and the Laws that Changed America*. New York: Houghton-Mifflin, 2005.

Rodriguez, Richard. *Hunger of Memory: The Education of Richard Rodriguez, An Autobiography*. New York: Random House, 1982.

U.S. Supreme Court, *Brown v. Board of Education*, 347 U.S. 483 (1954) (USSC+), 347 U.S. 483, Argued December 9, 1952, Reargued December 8, 1953, Decided May 17, 1954, Appeal From The United States District Court For The District Of Kansas.

U.S. Supreme Court, *Gratz et al. v. Bollinger et al.*, certiorari to the United States Court of Appeals for the Sixth Circuit, No. 02-516. Argued April 1, 2003. Decided June 23, 2003.

U.S. Supreme Court, *Plessy v. Ferguson*, 163 U.S. 537 (1896), 163 U.S. 537, No. 210.

FURTHER READING

McNeese, Tim. *Brown V. Board of Education (Great Supreme Court Decisions)*. New York: Chelsea House Publications, 2006.

Nolan, Han. *A Summer of Kings*. Orlando, Florida: Harcourt, 2006.

Patrick, Diane. *The New York Public Library Amazing African American History: A Book of Answers for Kids*. New York: John Wiley & Sons, Inc., 1998.

Rodriguez, Richard. *Hunger of Memory: The Education of Richard Rodriguez, An Autobiography*. New York: Random House, 1982.

Web Links

To learn more about affirmative action, visit ABDO Publishing Company on the World Wide Web at **www.abdopublishing.com**. Web sites about affirmative action are featured on our Book Links page. These links are routinely monitored and updated to provide the most current information available.

Places to Visit

U.S. Supreme Court
One First Street, NE, Washington, DC 20543
202-479-3211
www.cr.nps.gov/nr/travel/wash/dc78.htm
Tours, educational programs, and exhibits.

U.S. Capitol
Capitol Hill, Washington, DC 20543
202-225-6827
www.aoc.gov/cc/visit/index.cfm
Watch legislation in person. Obtain a pass to sit in the gallery of the U.S. Senate or the U.S. House of Representatives when they are in session.

National Archives
Constitution Avenue NW, Washington, DC 20408
202-357-5000
www.archives.gov/
View the Declaration of Independence, the U.S. Constitution, and the Bill of Rights.

Lyndon Baines Johnson Library and Museum
2313 Red River Street, Austin, TX 78705
512-721-0200
www.lbjlib.utexas.edu/
Radio and television remarks on signing the Civil Rights Bill, July 2, 1964.

Glossary

abolition
The official ending of slavery.

abridge
Diminish or lessen.

admissions criteria
The standards by which students are accepted to a school.

advocate
To support or promote a cause.

beneficiary
The person who receives a benefit.

benign
Non-threatening or harmless.

consent decree
A court agreement between two opposing groups.

controversial
Characterized by differing points of view.

creed
A religious belief.

desegregation
Integrating or putting together people of various backgrounds.

discriminatory
Treating a group unfairly because of prejudice about race, age, ability, etc.

diverse
Distinct qualities such as ethnicity, gender, or disability.

enfranchisement
Granting someone the privileges of citizenship, especially voting.

frivolous
Having no basis in law; of little importance legally.

impose
> To establish by authority such as a law or court.

initiative
> A plan designed to deal with a specific problem.

integration
> Combining groups regardless of race, class, or ethnic group.

interscholastic
> Exist or carry on between schools.

naturalize
> To give the rights of citizenship.

overt
> Open, undisguised.

pervasive
> To spread throughout.

plaintiff
> The person or group who brings a lawsuit against the defendant.

predominant
> The most common or most important.

provisional
> Temporary.

ratify
> To formally approve or confirm.

reaffirm
> To uphold a prior court decision.

reverse discrimination
> Discrimination against whites or males.

segregation
> The separation of a race, class, or ethnic group.

stipulations
> Conditions or requirements.

suffragist
> A woman who advocated voting rights for women.

SOURCE NOTES

Chapter 1. Leveling the Playing Field

1. Steve Mount. "United States Constitution." The U.S. Constitution Online, 6 June. 2007 <http://www.usconstitution.net/const.html#Am14>.
2. Steve Mount. "United States Constitution." The U.S. Constitution Online, 6 June 2007 <http://www.usconstitution.net/const.html#Am13>.
3. Firelight Media. "Brown Decision." *Beyond Brown: Pursing the Promise.* Public Broadcasting Service (PBS). 2004. 12 Feb. 2007.
4. Steve Mount. "United States Constitution." The U.S. Constitution Online, 6 June 2007. <http://www.usconstitution.net/const.html#Am19>.

Chapter 2. Should Affirmative Action Continue?

None.

Chapter 3. The Early Days of Affirmative Action

1. "Executive Order 8802. Reaffirming Participation In the Defense Program By All Persons, Regardless Of Race, Color, Or National Origin, And Directing Certain Action in Furtherance Of Said Policy." EEOC 35th Anniversary. 23 Mar. 2007 <http://www.eeoc.gov/abouteeoc/35th/thelaw/eo-8802.html>.
2. John F. Kennedy. "Executive Order 10925. Establishing the President's Committee On Equal Employment Opportunity." 6 Mar. 1961. 23 Mar. 2007 <http://www.eeoc.gov/abouteeoc/35th/thelaw/eo-10925.html>.
3. Nick Kotz. *Judgment Days: Lyndon Baines Johnson, Martin Luther King Jr., and the Laws that Changed America.* New York: Houghton-Mifflin, 2005. 334.
4. "Civil Rights Act of 1964, Document Number PL 88-352." 13 Aug. 1996. RBP Associates. 23 Mar. 2007 <http://usinfo.state.gov/usa/infousa/laws/majorlaw/civilr19.htm>.
5. "Executive Order 11246, As Amended. U.S. Department of Labor." 27 Mar. 2007 <http://www.dol.gov/esa/regs/statutes/ofccp/eo11246.htm>.

Chapter 4. Labor and Affirmative Action

None.

Chapter 5. *United States v. Paradise*

1. Cornell University Law School. The Legal Information Institute (LII). 6 June 2007 <http://www.law.cornell.edu/supct/html/historics/USSC_CR_0480_0149_ZS.html>.
2. Justia U.S. Supreme Court Center, United States V. Paradise, 480 U.S. 149 (1987), Justia.com U.S. Supreme Court Center. 29 Mar. 2007 <http://supreme.justia.com/us/480/149/case.html>.
3. Ibid.
4. Steve Mount. "United States Constitution." The U.S. Constitution Online, 6 June. 2007 <http://www.usconstitution.net/const.html#Am14>.
5. Justia U.S. Supreme Court Center, United States V. Paradise, 480 U.S. 149 (1987), Justia.com U.S. Supreme Court Center. 29 Mar. 2007 <http://supreme.justia.com/us/480/149/case.html>.
6. Justia U.S. Supreme Court Center, United States V. Paradise, 480 U.S. 149 (1987), Justia.com U.S. Supreme Court Center. 29 Mar. 2007 <http://supreme.justia.com/us/480/149/case.html>.
7. Ibid.
8. Ibid.

Chapter 6. Women and Affirmative Action

1. U.S. Department of Labor. "Title IX Education Amendments of 1972." 23 Mar. 2007 <http://www.dol.gov/oasam/regs/statutes/titleix.htm>.
2. Paul Halsall. "The Declaration of Sentiments, Seneca Falls Conference, 1848." *Modern History Sourcebook*. Nov.1998. 23 Mar. 2007 <http://www.fordham.edu/halsall/mod/Senecafalls.html>.
3. "Achieving Success Under Title IX." Title IX: 25 Years of Progress. 10 Jul. 1997. 23 Mar. 2007 <http://www.ed.gov/pubs/TitleIX/part5.html>.

SOURCE NOTES CONTINUED

Chapter 7. Minority Populations

1. U.S. Department of Labor. "Equal Opportunity for Individuals with Disabilities, Rehabilitation Act of 1973 as amended." Employment Law Guide. 20 Sept. 2005. 23 Mar. 2007 <http://www.dol.gov/compliance/guide/503.htm>.

Chapter 8. Higher Education and the U.S. Supreme Court

1. U.S. Department of Justice. Title VI of the Civil Rights Act of 1964, U.S. Department of Justice Coordination and Review Section, Civil Rights Division. 11 Apr. 2003. 23 Mar. 2007 <http://www.usdoj.gov/crt/cor/coord/titlevi.htm>.
2. Supreme Court Online. "*Gratz v. Bollinger.*" Duke Law. 6 June 2007 http://www.law.duke.edu/publiclaw/supremecourtonline/editedcases/pdf/gravbol.pdf.
3. Dr. Condoleezza Rice. "Statement by the National Security Advisor." The White House. 17 Jan. 2003. 23 Mar. 2007 <http://www.whitehouse.gov/news/releases/2003/01/print/20030117-1.html>.
4. President George W. Bush. *Remarks on the Michigan Affirmative Action Case.* The White House.15 Jan. 2003. 23 Mar. 2007 <http://www.whitehouse.gov/news/releases/2003/01/print/20030115-7.html>.
5. Supreme Court Online. "*Grutter v. Bollinger.*" Duke Law. 6 June 2007 <http://www.law.duke.edu/publiclaw/supremecourtonline/certgrants/2002/gruvbo>.

Chapter 9. Affirmative Action Experiences

1. U.S. Department of Labor. "Facts on Executive Order 11246— Affirmative Action." 4 Jan. 2002. 23. Mar. 2007 <http://www.dol.gov/esa/regs/compliance/ofccp/aa.htm>.
2. Richard Rodriguez. *Hunger of Memory: The Education of Richard Rodriguez, An Autobiography.* New York: Random House, 1982. 160.
3. Scott W. Williams. "On Affirmative Action." Topology Atlas. 10 May 1996. 23 Mar. 2007 <http://www.acsu.buffalo.edu/~sww/affirmact.html>.

4. Richard Rodriguez. *Hunger of Memory: The Education of Richard Rodriguez, An Autobiography.* New York: Random House, 1982. 153.
5. Ibid. 159.

Chapter 10. Yesterday, Today, and Tomorrow

1. William J. Clinton. "Mend It, Don't End It." Speech at National Archives. July 1995. 27 Mar. 2007 <http://www.americanreview.us/affirm1.htm>.
2. Mary Sue Coleman. Speech after Michigan voters approved Proposal 2. University of Michigan. 8 Nov. 2006. Regents of the University of Michigan. 25 Mar. 2007 <http://www.umich.edu/pres/speeches/061103div.html>.
3. William J. Clinton. "Mend It, Don't End It." Speech at National Archives. July 1995. 27 Mar. 2007 <http://www.americanreview.us/affirm1.htm>.

INDEX

ABOUT THE AUTHOR

M.J. Cosson has worked as an Information Specialist for the Iowa Department of Employment. She has also held several supervisory positions in publishing, hiring, and managing employees. She currently writes fiction and nonfiction books for children and young adults.

PHOTO CREDITS

Louie Balukoff/AP Images, cover, 3, 82; Matthias Kulka/zefa/Corbis, 6; AP Images, 12, 15, 24, 27, 33, 37, 41, 60, 63, 96, 97 (bottom); Chitose Suzuki/AP Images, 16, 99, (bottom); Karin Cooper/AP Images, 19; Danny Johnston/AP Images, 23; Marcy Nighswander/AP Images, 34; Stephen J. Boitano/AP Images, 42; Jupiterimages/AP Images, 51, 68, 97 (top); Susan B. Anthony House/AP Images, 52; South Bend Tribune, Marcus Marter/AP Images, 55; Tina Fineberg/AP Images, 59; Chet Brokaw/AP Images, 67; Walt Zeboski/AP Images, 73, 99 (top); The Mining Journal, Miriam Moeller/AP Images, 78, 98; Walt Zeboski/AP Images, 81; Noah Berger/AP Images, 89; Jim Bryant/AP Images, 90; The Berkshire Eagle, Ben Garver/AP Images, 95